General Dire

Adding sequins to even the most simple crochet design can completely change the appearance of your project. You can crochet with small sequins or large-hole paillettes for two totally different looks. Sequins may be added to each stitch for a glamorous, allover look or added here and there to add sparkle to your project.

Small-hole sequins are generally strung on thread rather than yarn. You may carry the thread along with any other yarn if you wish to use small sequins with another type of yarn.

Crocheting with small sequins is not a quick process but it is very simple to do. For ease in stringing, pour the sequins into a small bowl. This gives you a hard surface to push your needle against and will make it easier to pick up individual sequins.

Some small sequins are cupped. Be sure to insert your needle into the cupped side when stringing. This will ensure that the sequin faces in the proper direction when you crochet with it.

Photo A (small-hole sequins)

Large-hole sequins, also called paillettes, have the advantage of being easy to string onto most kinds of yarns or threads.

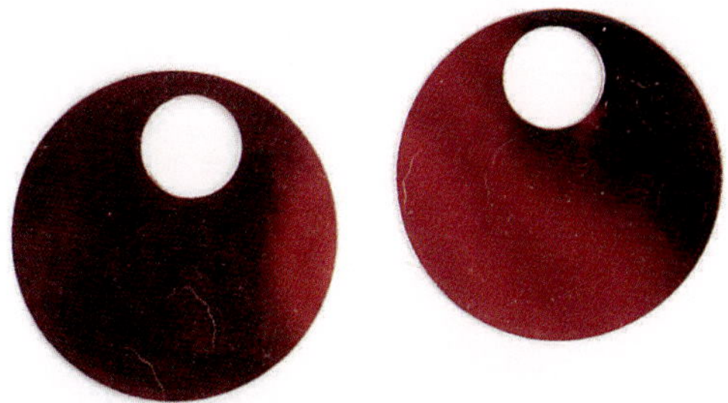

Photo B (large-hole sequins)

Sequ

To plac... sequin into place against the last chain stitch made (Photo C). Bring yarn over hook on other side of sequin (Photo D) and pull through loop on hook. Sequin will fall to back of work (Photo E).

Photo C

Photo D

Photo E

Sequins in Single Crochet

To place a sequin after a single crochet, slide sequin into place against the last single crochet made (Photo F). Work next stitch as instructed. Sequin falls to back of single crochet (Photo G).

When the piece is completed, the side with the sequins is the right side of the piece.

Photo F

Photo G

Sequins in Double Crochet

To place a sequin after a double crochet stitch, slide sequin into place against the last double crochet made (Photo H). Work next stitch as instructed. Sequin falls to back of work (Photo I).

When the piece is completed, the side with the sequins is the right side of the piece.

Photo H

Photo I

Paillette Triple Crochet

In the Touch of Sparkle Jacket pattern, a Paillette Triple Crochet stitch is used that has the paillette worked into the triple crochet stitch.

To work a paillette into a triple crochet stitch, yarn over twice, insert hook in stitch or space indicated and draw loop through, [yarn over, draw through 2 loops on hook] twice, slide paillette into place next to the loop just made (Photo J). Bring yarn over hook, making sure the paillette is captured in this yarn over and is on the back of the stitch (Photo K). Yarn over and pull through 2 loops to complete stitch (Photo L).

Photo J

Photo K

Photo L

Fab Flower Pin

EASY

Size

2 x 3 inches

Materials

- DMC Senso Microfiber Cotton size 3 thread (150 yds per ball):
  2 yds each #1104 light pink, #1105 pink, #1110 blue, #1108 green
- Size E/4/3.5mm crochet hook or size needed to obtain gauge
- Tapestry needle
- 10mm cupped sequins:
  6 fuchsia
  3 green
- Pin backing
- Sewing needle

Gauge

Rnds 1–3 = 1¾ inches

Instructions

Note: *With sewing needle, string fuchsia sequins on pink thread, pushing through cupped side. String green sequins on green thread.*

Flower

Rnd 1 (WS): With pink, ch 4, join to form ring, ch 1, [sc in ring, slide sequin up] 6 times, join in first sc.

Rnd 2: Ch 1, in same sc as joining and in each rem sc work (sc, ch 2, sc), join in first sc. Turn.

Rnd 3 (RS): Sl st in next ch-2 sp, ch 1, in same sp work (sc, 3 dc, sc), ch 1, [in next ch-2 sp work (sc, 3 dc, sc), ch 1] 5 times, join in first sc. Fasten off.

Rnd 4: Hold piece with RS facing you, join light pink in any ch-1 sp, sl st in next st, [ch 1, sl st in next st] 4 times, ***sl st in next ch-1 sp, sl st in next st, [ch 1, sl st in next st] 4 times, rep from * 4 times more; join in same sp as first sl st made. (*36 sl sts*)

Rnd 5: Hold piece with RS facing you, working over sl sts of previous rnd, with blue, make slip knot on hook and join with sc in any ch-1 sp on rnd 3, ch 3, in same sp work [sc, ch 3] twice, sc in same sp, *in next ch-1 sp work [sc, ch 3] 3 times, sc in same sp, rep from * around, join in first sc.

Fasten off and weave in all ends.

Leaf

Make 3.

With green, ch 5, sc in 2nd ch from hook, slide sequin up, ch 1, sc in same ch, dc in next ch, hdc in next ch, in next ch work (sc, ch 3, sc in 3rd ch from hook, sc), working in unused lps on opposite side of beg ch, hdc in next lp, dc in next lp, join in first sc.

Fasten off, leaving a 8-inch end for sewing.

Finishing

Step 1: Referring to photo for placement and with tapestry needle and matching thread, sew Leaves to Flower.

Step 2: With tapestry needle and matching thread, sew pin backing to back of Flower.

Stardust Shawl

Size

One size

Materials

- Aunt Lydia's Double Strand crochet cotton (300 yds per ball): 2 balls #444 ocean/aqua *(A)*
- South Maid size 10 crochet cotton (300 yds per ball): 2 balls #995 ocean *(B)*
- Size G/6/4mm crochet hook or size needed to obtain gauge
- Tapestry needle
- 1,890 clear iridescent 10mm cupped sequins
- Sewing needle

Gauge

With 1 strand of A and B held tog in pattern, tr, ch 3, tr = 1 inch

Instructions

Note: *With sewing needle, string half of sequins on B, pushing through cupped side.*

First Panel

Row 1 (RS): With 1 strand of A and B held tog, ch 68, tr in 11th ch from hook *(beg 10 sk chs count as a 3 sk chs, tr and ch-3 sp)*, *ch 3, sk next 3 chs, tr in next ch, rep from * across, turn. *(16 tr)*

Row 2: Ch 4 *(counts as a tr on this and following rnds)*, *[slide sequin up, ch 1] 3 times, tr in next tr, rep from * to beg 10 sk chs, [slide sequin up, ch 1] 3 times, sk next 3 chs of beg 10 sk chs, tr in next ch, turn.

Row 3: Ch 7 *(counts as a tr and a ch-3 sp on this and following rows)*, tr in next tr, *ch 3, tr in next tr, rep from * to turning ch-4, ch 3, tr in 4th ch of turning ch-4, turn.

Row 4: Ch 4, *[slide sequin up, ch 1] 3 times, tr in next tr, rep from * to turning ch-7, [slide sequin up, ch 1] 3 times, sk next 3 chs of turning ch-7, tr in next ch, turn.

Rows 5–50: [Work rows 3 and 4] 23 times.

Row 51: Rep row 3.

Fasten off and weave in ends.

Second Panel

Note: *String rem sequins on B.*

Row 1 (WS): Hold piece with WS facing you and beg ch to right, with strand of A and B held tog and working in ends of row ends, join in base of last tr on row 1, ch 7, tr in top of same tr on row 1, [ch 3, tr in top of first st on next row] 14 times, turn.

Row 2 (RS): Ch 4, *[slide sequin up and hold to front of work, ch 1] 3 times, tr in next tr, rep from * to beg ch-7, [slide sequin up and hold to front of work, ch 1] 3 times, sk next 3 chs of beg ch-7, tr in next ch, turn.

Row 3: Ch 7, tr in next tr, *ch 3, tr in next tr, rep from * to turning ch-4, ch 3, tr in 4th ch of turning ch-4, turn.

Row 4: Ch 4, *[slide sequin up and hold to front of work, ch 1] 3 times, tr in next tr, rep from * to turning ch-7, [slide sequin up and hold to front of work, ch 1] 3 times, sk next 3 chs of turning ch-7, tr in next ch, turn.

Rows 5–34: [Work rows 3 and 4] 15 times.

Row 35: Rep row 3.

Fasten off and weave in ends.

Fringe

Cut 20-inch strands of A and B. Use 3 strands each of A and B for each knot. Fold strands in half and draw folded end through from back to front. Pull ends through folded end and tighten knot. Working in sps formed by end sts of rows along outer edge, sk first 14 rows, tie knot in every other row around outer edge, skipping last 14 rows on opposite end. Trim ends even.

Purple Haze Scarf

Size

17 x 72 inches

Materials

- Red Heart Symphony medium (worsted) weight yarn (3½ oz/310 yds/100g per skein): 2 skeins #4903 mystic purple
- Size K/10½/6.5mm crochet hook or size needed to obtain gauge
- Tapestry needle
- 528 Sulyn large-hole pink paillettes

Gauge

In pattern, 4 sc and 3 ch sps = 5¼ inches

Instructions

Note: *With tapestry needle, string one-half of paillettes on each skein of yarn.*

Row 1: Ch 38, sc in 2nd ch from hook and in each rem ch, turn. *(37 sc)*

Row 2: Ch 1, sc in first sc, *****ch 4, sk next 2 sc, sc in next sc, rep from ***** across, turn. *(13 sc)*

Row 3: Ch 1, sc in first sc, ch 2, sc in next ch-4 sp, *****ch 2, slide paillette up, ch 2, sc in next ch-4 sp, rep from ***** to last sc, ch 2, sc in last sc, turn. *(14 sc)*

Row 4: Ch 1, sc in first sc, *****ch 4, sc in next ch-4 sp (before paillette), rep from ***** to last sc, ch 4, sc in last sc, turn. *(13 sc)*

Rows 5–98: [Work rows 3 and 4] 47 times.

Row 99: Ch 1, sc in first sc, *****2 sc in next ch-4 sp, sc in next sc, rep from ***** across.

Fasten off and weave in ends.

Purple Haze Tunic

Sizes

Woman's small (medium, large, X-large, 2X) Pattern is written for smallest size with changes for larger sizes in brackets.

Finished Garment Measurements

36¼ inches (*small*) [40½ inches (*medium*), 44¾ inches (*large*), 49 inches (*X-large*), 53¼ inches (*2X*)]

Materials

- Red Heart Symphony medium (worsted) weight yarn (3½ oz/310 yds/100g per ball): 4 (5, 5, 6, 6) skeins #4903 mystic purple
- Size K/10½/6.5mm crochet hook or size needed to obtain gauge
- Tapestry needle
- 636 (675, 838, 887, 1064) Sulyn large-hole pink paillettes

Gauge

In pattern, 4 sc and 3 ch sps = 5¼ inches

Instructions

Note: *With tapestry needle, string 160 paillettes on yarn. String rem paillettes as needed.*

Body

Rnd 1 (WS): Ch 79 [88, 97,106, 115], sc in 2nd ch from hook and in each rem ch, join in first sc, turn. *(78 [87, 96, 105, 114] sc)*

Rnd 2: Ch 1, sc in first sc, *ch 4, sk next 2 sc, sc in next sc, rep from * to last 2 sc, ch 4, sk last 2 sc, join in first sc, turn. *(26 [29, 32, 35, 38] ch-4 sps)*

Rnd 3: Sl st in next ch-4 sp, ch 1, sc in same sp, ch 2, slide paillette up, ch 2, *sc in next ch-4 sp, ch 2, slide paillette up, ch 2, rep from * around, join in first sc, turn.

Rnd 4: Sl st in next ch-4 sp, ch 1, sc in same sp, ch 4, *sc in next ch-4 sp (before paillette), ch 4, rep from * around, join in first sc, turn.

Rnds 5–24: [Work rnds 3 and 4] ten times.

Rnd 25: Rep rnd 3.

Front

Row 1: Ch 1, sc in first sc, ch 2, sc in next ch-4 sp (before paillette), [ch 4, sc in next ch-4 sp (before paillette)] 11 [12, 14, 15, 17] times, ch 2, sc in next sc, turn, leaving rem ch-4 sps unworked. *(14 [15, 17, 18, 20] sc)*

Row 2: Ch 1, sc in first sc, ch 2, slide paillette up, ch 2, *sc in next ch-4 sp, ch 2, slide paillette up, ch 2, rep from * to last sc, sc in last sc, turn. *(13 [14, 16, 17, 19] sc)*

Row 3: Ch 1, sc in first sc, ch 2, sc in next ch-4 sp (before paillette), [ch 4, sc in next ch-4 sp (before paillette)] 11 [12, 14, 15, 17] times, ch 2, sc in last sc, turn.

Rows 4–9 (4-9, 4-11, 4-11, 4-13): [Work rows 2 and 3] 3 (3, 5, 5, 7) times.

First Shoulder

Row 1: Ch 1, sc in first sc, ch 2, slide paillette up, ch 2, [sc in next ch-4 sp, ch 2, slide paillette up, ch 2] twice, sc in next ch-4 sp, turn, leaving rem ch-4 sps unworked. *(4 sc)*

Row 2: Ch 1, sc in first sc, ch 2, sc in next ch-4 sp (before paillette), [ch 4, sc in next ch-4 sp (before paillette)] twice, ch 2, sc in next sc, turn. *(5 sc)*

Row 3: Ch 1, sc in first sc, ch 2, slide paillette up, ch 2, [sc in next ch-4 sp, ch 2, slide paillette up, ch 2] twice, sc in next sc, turn. *(4 sc)*

For Sizes Small & Medium Only

Rows 4 & 5: Rep rows 2 and 3. At end of row 5, fasten off.

Continue with 2nd Shoulder.

For Size Large Only

Rows 4–7: [Work rows 2 and 3] twice. At end of row 7, fasten off.

Continue with 2nd Shoulder.

For Sizes X-large & 2X Only

Rows 4–9: [Work rows 2 and 3] 3 times. At end of row 9, fasten off.

Continue with 2nd Shoulder.

2nd Shoulder

Row 1: Hold piece with RS facing you, sk next 6 ch-4 sps on front from First Shoulder, make slip knot on hook and join with sc in next ch-4 sp, ch 2, slide paillette up, ch 2, [sc in next ch-4 sp, ch 2, slide paillette up, ch 2] twice, sc in last sc, turn. *(4 sc)*

For Sizes Small & Medium Only

Rows 2–5: Rep rows 2–5 of First Shoulder. At end of row 5, fasten off.

Weave in all ends.

Continue with Back.

For Size Large Only

Rows 2–7: Rep rows 2–7 of First Shoulder. At end of row 7, fasten off.

Weave in all ends.

Continue with Back.

For Sizes X-large & 2X Only

Rows 4–9: Rep rows 2–9 of First Shoulder. At end of row 9, fasten off.

Weave in all ends.

Continue with Back.

Back

Row 1: Hold piece with RS facing you, sk next unused ch-4 sp on Body from 2nd Shoulder, make slip knot on hook and join with sc in next st, ch 2, sc in next ch-4 sp (before paillette), [ch 4, sc in next ch-4 sp (before paillette)] 11 [13, 14, 16, 17] times, ch 2, sc in next sc, turn, leaving rem ch-4 sp unworked. *(14 [14, 13, 17, 16] sc)*

Rows 2–9 [2–9, 2–11, 2–11, 2–13]: Rep rows 2–9 [2–9, 2–11, 2–11, 2–13] of Front.

Fasten off and weave in ends.

Assembly

With tapestry needle, sew shoulder seams, matching corresponding sts and ch-4 sps of last row of First and 2nd Shoulders to sts on last row of Back.

Sleeve

Make 2.

Rnd 1 (RS): Hold piece with RS facing you, join in sk ch-4 sp at bottom of 1 armhole, ch 1, sc in same sp, ch 4, working around armhole in ends of rows of Front and Back, work (sc, ch 4) 9 [9, 11, 11, 13] times evenly spaced, join in first sc, turn.

Rnd 2: Sl st in next ch-4 sp, ch 1, sc in same sp, ch 2, slide paillette up, ch 2, *sc in next ch-4 sp, ch 2, slide paillette up, ch 2, rep from * around; join in first sc, turn.

Rnd 3: Sl st in next ch-4 sp (before paillette), ch 1, sc in same sp, ch 4, *sc in next ch-4 sp (before paillette), ch 4, rep from * around; join in first sc, turn.

Rnds 4–27: [Work rnds 2 and 3] 12 times.

Rnd 28: Rep rnd 2.

Edging

Rnd 1: Sl st in next ch-4 sp (before paillette), ch 1, sc in same sp, ch 1, *sc in next ch-4 sp (before paillette), ch 1, rep from * around; join in first sc, turn.

Rnd 2: Ch 1, sc in first sc, in each ch-1 sp and in each sc, join in first sc, turn.

Rnd 3: Ch 1, sc in each sc, join in first sc, turn.

Rnd 4: Ch 1, sc in each sc, join in first sc.

Fasten off and weave in ends.

Neck Edging

Rnd 1 (RS): Hold piece with RS facing you, make slip knot on hook and join with sc in first skipped ch-4 sp on Front, ch 1, [sc in next ch-4 sp, ch 1] 4 [5, 7, 8, 10] times, working in ends of rows of next shoulder, [sk next row, sc in next row, ch 1] 2 [2, 3, 4, 4] times, working across Back, [sc in next ch-4 sp, ch 1] 5 [6, 8, 9, 11] times, working in ends of rows of next shoulder, [sk next row, sc in next row, ch 1] 2 [2, 3, 4, 4] times, join in first sc.

Rnd 2: Ch 1, sc in same sc, in each ch-1 sp and in each rem sc, join in first sc.

Rnd 3 & 4: Ch 1, sc in same sc and in each rem sc, join in first sc.

Fasten off and weave in ends.

Ruby Evening Bag

EASY

Size

7 x 8 inches, excluding handle

Materials

- Aunt Lydia's Classic Crochet size 10 crochet cotton (350 yds per ball):
  1 ball #494 victory red *(A)*
- Red Heart Lustersheen fine (sport) weight yarn (4 oz/335 yds/113g per skein):
  1 skein #0915 cherry red *(B)*
- Size G/6/4mm crochet hook or size needed to obtain gauge
- Tapestry needle
- 1,222 red 8mm cupped sequins
- Purchased purse handle, 6½ x 5 inches
- 1 snap
- Sewing needle

Gauge

With 1 strand of A and B held tog, 13 sc = 3 inches

Instructions

Note: *With sewing needle, string sequins on A, pushing through cupped side.*

Front

Row 1 (RS): With 1 strand of A and B held tog, ch 28, sc in 2nd ch from hook and in each rem ch, turn. *(27 sc)*

Row 2: Ch 1, sc in first sc, ***slide sequin up, sc in next sc, rep from * across, turn.

Row 3: Ch 1, sc in each sc, turn.

Rows 4–37: [Work rows 2 and 3] 17 times. At end of row 37, fasten off.

Back

Row 1: Hold Front with RS facing you and beg ch at top, working in unused lps of beg ch, make slip knot on hook and join with sc in first unused lp and in each rem unused lp, turn. *(27 sc)*

Rows 2–37: Rep rows 2–37 of Front. At end of last row, do not fasten off.

Flap

Row 1: Ch 1, sc in first sc, ***slide sequin up, sc in next sc, rep from * across, turn.

Row 2: Ch 1, sc in each sc, turn.

Rows 3–22: [Work rows 1 and 2] 10 times.

Fasten off and weave in all ends.

Finishing

With tapestry needle and A, sew side seams. With sewing needle and matching thread, sew snap to WS of center of flap and to row 30 on Front. Referring to photo for placement, sew handle to bag.

Gold Dust Belt

EASY

Size

1¼ inches x desired length

Materials

- Lion Brand Glitterspun medium (worsted) weight yarn (1¾ oz/115 yds/50g per skein): 1 skein #170 gold *(A)*

4 MEDIUM

- Royale Metallic Crochet size 10 crochet cotton (100 yds per ball): 1 ball #90G gold/gold *(B)*
- Size G/6/4mm crochet hook or size needed to obtain gauge
- Tapestry needle
- 8mm gold sequins (1 for each 1¼ inches of desired length)
- 1-inch buckle
- Sewing needle

Gauge

With 1 strand of A and B held tog, 3 sts = 1¼ inches

Instructions

Note: *With sewing needle, string all sequins on B, pushing through cupped side.*

Center

Row 1 (RS): With 1 strand of A and B held tog, ch 6, dc in 5th ch from hook, working over dc just made, dc in previous ch, dc in last ch, turn.

Row 2: Ch 3 *(counts as a dc on this and following rows)*, sk next dc, dc in next dc, slide sequin up, working over dc just made, dc in sk dc, dc in 3rd ch of beg 3 sk chs, turn.

Row 3: Ch 3, sk next dc, dc in next dc, working over dc just made, dc in sk dc, dc in 3rd ch of turning ch-3, turn.

Row 4: Ch 3, sk next dc, dc in next dc, slide sequin up, working over dc just made, dc in sk dc, dc in 3rd ch of turning ch-3, turn.

Rep rows 3 and 4 for desired length, ending with a row 3.

Fasten off and weave in ends.

Edging

Hold piece with RS facing you and 1 long edge at top, with 1 strand of A and B held tog, make slip knot on hook and join with sc in end of first row in upper right-hand corner, sc in same row, working in ends of rows, 2 sc in each rem row. Fasten off. Rep on rem long edge. Weave in ends.

Finishing

With tapestry needle and A, sew buckle pieces to ends of belt.

Gold Rush Camisole

EASY

Sizes

Woman's small [medium, large, X-large, 2X] Pattern is written for smallest size with changes for larger sizes in brackets.

Finished Garment Measurements

36 inches (*small*) [40 inches (*medium*), 44 inches (*large*), 48 inches (*X-large*), 52 inches (*2X*)]

Materials

- TLC Amore medium (worsted) weight yarn (6 oz/290 yds/170g per skein): 2 (2, 3, 3, 3) skeins #3220 wheat *(A)*

4 MEDIUM

- Aunt Lydia's Classic Crochet Thread size 10 crochet cotton (350 yds per ball): 1 ball #421 goldenrod *(B)*
- Size I/9/5.5mm crochet hook or size needed to obtain gauge
- Tapestry needle
- 435 (480, 525, 570, 615) gold 8mm sequins
- Sewing needle

Gauge

In pattern, 6 sts = 4 inches

Special Stitches

Cross st (X-st): Sk st indicated, dc in next st, working over dc just made, dc in sk st.

Front post double crochet (fpdc): Yo, insert hook from front to back to front around post (see Stitch Guide) of st indicated, draw lp through, [yo, draw through 2 lps on hook] twice.

Instructions

Rnd 1 (RS): Starting at bottom with A, ch 88 [97, 106, 115, 124], sc in 2nd ch from hook and in each rem ch, join in first sc. *(87 [96, 105, 114, 123] sc)*

Rnd 2: Ch 3 (*counts as a dc on this and following rnds*), dc in each rem sc, join in 3rd ch of beg ch-3.

Rnd 3: Ch 3, **X-st** *(see Special Stitches)* over next 2 dc, **fpdc** *(see Special Stitches)* around next dc, X-st over next 2 dc, *fpdc around next dc, X-st over next 2 dc, rep from * around; join in 3rd ch of beg ch-3. *(58 [64, 70, 76, 82] sts)*

Rnds 3–26: Rep rnd 3. At end of last rnd, turn.

Edging

Note: *With sewing needle, string all sequins on B, pushing through cupped side.*

Rnd 1: With 1 strand of A and B held tog, ch 1, sc in first dc, slide sequin up, *sc in next dc, slide sequin up, rep from* around; join in first sc. *(87 [96, 105, 114, 123) sc)*

Rnd 2: Ch 1, sc in first sc, slide sequin up, *sc in next sc, slide sequin up, rep from* around; join in first sc.

Rnds 3–5: Rep rnd 2.

Rnd 6: Ch 1, sc in each sc.

Fasten off and weave in ends.

Strap

Make 2.

Row 1: With A, ch 41 [43, 45, 47, 49], sc in 2nd ch from hook and in each rem ch, turn. *(40 [42, 44, 46, 48] sc)*

Row 2: Ch 1, sl st in each st across.

Fasten off and weave in ends.

Finishing

With tapestry needle and A, sew end of 1 strap to any 2 sc on rnd 6. For first armhole, sk next 25 (26, 27, 28, 29) sc, sew opposite end of strap to next 2 sc. Sk next 14 (18, 21, 25, 28) sc, sew 1 end of 2nd strap to next 2 sc. For 2nd armhole, sk next 25 [26, 27, 28, 29] sc, sew opposite end of strap to next 2 sc.

Sapphires & Pearls Scrunchie/Bracelet

EASY

Size

One size

Materials

- Aunt Lydia's Classic Crochet size 3 cotton thread (150 yds per ball):
  1 ball #175 warm blue
- Size G/6/4mm crochet hook or size needed to obtain gauge
- Tapestry needle
- Elastic hair band
- 32 white 6mm pearls
- 16 blue pony beads
- 16 blue 12mm sequins

Gauge

Gauge not important for this project.

Instructions

Note: *Sring pearls, beads and sequins on thread in following sequence: pearl, pony bead, pearl, sequin.*

Make slip knot on hook and join with sc over elastic band, *slide pearl up, sc over elastic band, ch 1, slide pony bead up, ch 1, sc over elastic band, slide pearl up, sc over elastic band, ch 2, slide sequin up, ch 2, sc over elastic band, rep from * 14 times more; slide pearl up, sc over elastic band, ch 1, slide pony bead up, ch 1, sc over elastic band, slide pearl up, sc over elastic band, ch 2, slide sequin up, ch 2, join in joining sc.

Fasten off and weave in ends.

Luminous Belt

EASY

Size

1½ inches x desired length

Materials

- Lion Brand Glitterspun medium (worsted) weight yarn (1¾ oz/115 yds/50g per skein): 1 skein #150 silver *(A)*
- Royale Metallic Crochet size 10 crochet cotton (100 yds per ball): 1 ball #410S silver/silver *(B)*
- Size G/6/4mm crochet hook or size needed to obtain gauge
- Tapestry needle
- 8mm silver sequins (10 for each 1 inch of desired length)
- 1-inch buckle
- Sewing needle

4 MEDIUM

Gauge

With 1 strand of A and B held tog, 6 sc = 1½ inches

Instructions

Note: *With sewing needle, string all sequins on B, pushing through cupped side.*

Row 1 (RS): With 1 strand of A and B held tog, ch 7, sc in 2nd ch from hook and in each rem ch, turn.

Row 2: Ch 1, sc in first sc, [slide sequin up, sc in next sc] 5 times, turn.

Row 3: Ch 1, sc in each sc, turn.

Rep rows 2 and 3 twice for each additional inch of length.

Fasten off and weave in ends.

Finishing

With tapestry needle and A, sew buckle pieces to ends of belt.

Sparkling Violet Scrunchie/Bracelet

Size

One size

Materials

- Aunt Lydia's Classic Crochet size 10 crochet cotton (350 yds per ball):
  1 ball #458 purple
- Size G/6/4mm crochet hook or size needed to obtain gauge
- Tapestry needle
- Elastic hair band
- 36 clear 10mm plastic jewels
- 36 (12mm) sequins in assorted pink, clear and purple
- Sewing needle

Gauge

Gauge not important for this project

Instructions

***Note:** With sewing needle, string jewels and sequins on thread in following sequence: 3 jewels, 3 sequins.*

Make slip knot on hook and join with sc over elastic band, *****[ch 1, slide jewel up, ch 2, sc over elastic band] 3 times, [ch 2, slide sequin up] 3 times, ch 2, sc in last sc made, sc over elastic band, rep from ***** 10 times more; [ch 1, slide jewel up, ch 2, sc over elastic band] 3 times, [ch 2, slide sequin up] 3 times, ch 2, sc in last sc made, join in joining sc.

Fasten off and weave in ends.

Flip-Flops with Flair

EASY

Size

One size fits most

Materials

- Red Heart Plush medium (worsted) weight yarn (6 oz/278 yds/170g per skein): 10 yds #9752 grenadine
- Size I/9/5.5mm crochet hook or size needed to obtain gauge
- Tapestry needle
- 76 pink metallic pony beads
- 38 Sulyn large-hole fuchsia paillettes

4 MEDIUM

Gauge

Gauge not important for this project.

Instructions

Note: *With tapestry needle, string pony beads and paillettes in following sequence: 2 pony beads, 1 paillette.*

Hold 1 flip-flop with heel toward you, make slip knot on hook and join with sc around left strap near heel, 2 sc around strap, [slide 2 beads and 1 paillette up, ch 1, 3 sc around strap] 9 times, sk thong, working up right strap, [slide 2 beads and 1 paillette up, ch 1, 3 sc around strap] 10 times.

Fasten off and weave in ends.

Rep on 2nd flip-flop.

Chances Are Shawl

EASY

Size

24 x 63 inches

Materials

- Lion Brand Trellis super bulky (super chunky) weight yarn (1¾ oz/115 yds/50g per ball):
  7 balls #304 rainbow (*A*)
- South Maid size 10 crochet cotton (350 yds per ball):
  2 balls #12 black (*B*)
- Size N/13/9mm crochet hook or size needed to obtain gauge
- Tapestry needle
- 504 multicolored paillettes
- Sewing needle

Gauge

With 1 strand of A and B held tog, 2 dc = 1 inch

Special Stitch

Cross stitch (X-st): Sk st indicated, dc in next st, working over dc just made, dc in sk st.

Instructions

Note: *With sewing needle, string 252 sequins on each ball of B.*

Row 1 (RS): With 1 strand of A and B held tog, ch 49, sc in 2nd ch from hook and in each rem ch, turn.

Row 2: Ch 3 (*counts as a dc on this and following rows*), dc in next sc, *slide sequin up, ch 1, dc in next 2 sc, rep from * across, turn. (*48 dc*)

Row 3: Ch 3, **X-st** (*see Special Stitch*) over next 2 dc, *X-st over next 2 dc, rep from * to turning ch-3, dc in 3rd ch of turning ch-3.

Row 4: Ch 1, sc in first dc, *ch 3, sk next X-st, sc in sp before next X-st, rep from * to last X-st, ch 3, sk last X-st, sc in 3rd ch of turning ch-3, turn.

Row 5: Ch 3, 2 dc in each ch-3 sp, dc in last sc, turn. (*48 dc*)

Rows 6–81: [Work rows 2–5] 19 times.

Row 82: Rep row 2.

Row 83: Ch 1, sc in each dc and in 3rd ch of turning ch-3.

Fasten off and weave in all ends.

Fringe

Cut 22-inch strands of A. Use 2 strands for each knot. Fold strands in half and draw folded end from back to front through first sc of row 83. Pull ends through folded end and tighten knot. Tie knot in each rem sc of row 83 and in each unused lp of beg ch on opposite end. Trim ends even.

Touch of Sparkle Jacket

EASY

Sizes

Woman's small [medium, large, X-large, 2X] Pattern is written for smallest size with changes for larger sizes in brackets.

Finished Garment Measurements

34¼ inches (*small*) [38¾ inches (*medium*), 43¼ inches (*large*), 47¾ inches (*X-large*), 52¼ inches (*2X*)]

Materials

- Red Heart Super Saver medium (worsted) weight yarn (7 oz/364 yds/198g per skein): 2 (3, 3, 4, 4) skeins #0778 lt fuchsia
- Size K/10½/6.5mm crochet hook or size needed to obtain gauge
- Tapestry needle
- 225 Sulyn large-hole fuchsia paillettes

Gauge

6 sts and 2 ch-1 sps = 3 inches

Special Stitch

Paillette triple crochet (paillette tr): Yo twice, insert hook in sp indicated and draw lp through, [yo, draw through 2 lps on hook] twice, slide paillette up, yo and draw through 2 lps on hook.

Instructions

Back

Row 1 (WS): Starting at top, ch 53 [57, 61, 65, 69], dc in 4th ch from hook and in next ch (*beg 3 sk chs count as a dc*), [ch 1, sk next ch, dc in next 3 chs] 12 [13, 14, 15, 16] times, turn. (*39 [42, 45, 48, 51] dc*)

Row 2 (RS): Ch 1, sc in first dc, *ch 4, sc in next ch-1 sp, rep from * to last 3 dc and beg 3 sk chs; ch 4, sk next 2 dc, sc in 3rd ch of beg 3 sk chs, turn. (*14 [15, 16, 17, 18] sc*)

Row 3: Sl st in next ch-4 sp, ch 3 (*counts as a dc on this and following rows*), 2 dc in same sp, *ch 1, 3 dc in next ch-4 sp, rep from * across; turn. (*39 [42, 45, 48, 51] dc*)

Rows 4–19: [Work rows 2 and 3] 8 times.

Row 20: Sl st in first 3 dc and in next ch-1 sp, ch 1, sc in same sp, *ch 4, sc in next ch-1 sp, rep from * to last ch-1 sp; turn, leaving rem sts unworked. (*12 [13, 14, 15, 16] sc*)

Row 21: Rep row 3. (*33 [36, 39, 42, 45] dc at end of row*)

Row 22: Rep row 20. (*10 [11, 12, 13, 14] sc at end of row*)

Row 23: Rep row 3. (*27 [30, 33, 36, 39] dc at end of row*)

Row 24: Rep row 20. (*8 [9, 10, 11, 12] sc at end of row*)

Row 25: Rep row 3. (*21 [24, 27, 30, 33] dc at end of row*)

Fasten off and weave in ends.

Right Front Shoulder

For Size Small Only

Row 1: Hold Back with RS facing you and beg ch at top, join in first unused lp of beg ch, ch 3 (*counts as a dc on this and following rows*), working in rem unused lps of beg ch, dc in next 2 lps, [ch 1, sk next lp, dc in next 3 lps] 3 times, turn, leaving rem lps unworked. (*12 dc*)

For Size Medium Only

Row 1: Hold Back with RS facing you and beg ch at top, join in first unused lp of beg ch, ch 3 (*counts as a dc on this and following rows*), dc in same lp, working in rem unused lps of beg ch, dc in next lp, ch 1, sk next lp, 2 dc in next lp, dc in next lp, [ch 1, sk next lp, dc in next 3 lps] 3 times, turn, leaving rem lps unworked. (*15 dc*)

Continue with For All Sizes.

For Size Large Only

Row 1: Hold Back with RS facing you and beg ch at top, join in first unused lp of beg ch, ch 3 (*counts as a dc on this and following rows*), dc in same lp, working in rem unused lps of beg ch, dc in next lp, ch 1, sk next lp, 2 dc in next lp, dc in next lp, [ch 1, sk next lp, dc in next 3 lps] twice, [ch 1, sk next lp, dc in next lp, 2 dc in next lp] twice, turn, leaving rem lps unworked. (*18 dc*)

Continue with For All Sizes.

For Size X-large Only

Row 1: Hold Back with RS facing you and beg ch at top, join in first unused lp of beg ch, ch 3 (*counts as a dc on this and following rows*), working in rem unused lps of beg ch, dc in next 2 lps, [ch 1, sk next lp, 2 dc in next lp, dc in next lp] 6 times, turn, leaving rem lps unworked. (*21 dc*)

Continue with For All Sizes.

For Size 2X Only

Row 1: Hold Back with RS facing you and beg ch at top, join in first unused lp of beg ch, ch 3 (*counts as a dc on this and following rows*), dc in same lp, working in rem unused lps of beg ch, dc in next lp, [ch 1, sk next lp, 2 dc in next lp, dc in next lp] 7 times, turn, leaving rem lps unworked. (*24 dc*)

Continue with For All Sizes.

For All Sizes

Row 2: Ch 1, sc in first dc, *ch 4, sc in next ch-1 sp, rep from * to last 2 dc and beg ch-3; ch 4, sk last 2 dc, sc in 3rd ch of beg ch-3, turn. (5 [6, 7, 8, 9] sc)

Row 3: Sl st in next ch-4 sp, ch 3, 2 dc in same sp, *ch 1, 3 dc in next ch-4 sp, rep from * across; turn. *(12 [15, 18, 21, 24] dc)*

Rows 4–9 [4–9, 4–9, 4–11, 4–11]: [Work rows 2 and 3] 3 [3, 3, 4, 4] times.

Row 10 [10, 10, 12, 12]: Sl st in first 3 dc and in next ch-1 sp, ch 1, sc in same sp, *ch 4, sc in next ch-1 sp, rep from * to last 2 dc and turning ch-3; ch 4, sk last 2 dc, sc in 3rd ch of turning ch-3, turn. *(4 [5, 6, 7, 8] sc)*

Row 11 [11, 11, 13, 13]: Rep row 3. *(9 [12, 15, 18, 21] dc)*

Row 12 [12, 12, 14, 14]: Rep row 10 [10, 10, 12, 12]. *(3 [4, 5, 6, 7] sc)*

Row 13 [13, 13, 15, 15]: Rep row 3. *(6 [9, 12, 15, 18] dc)*

Fasten off and weave in ends.

Left Front Shoulder

For Size Small Only

Row 1: Hold Back with RS facing you and beg ch at top, sk next 21 unused lps of beg ch from Right Front Shoulder, join in next lp, ch 3, working in rem unused lps of beg ch, dc in next 2 lps, [ch 1, sk next lp, dc in next 3 lps] 3 times, turn. *(12 dc)*

Continue with For All Sizes.

For Size Medium Only

Row 1: Hold Back with RS facing you and beg ch at top, skip next 21 unused lps of beg ch from Right Front Shoulder, join in next lp, ch 3, dc in next 2 lps, [ch 1, sk next lp, dc in next 3 lps] twice, [ch 1, sk next lp, dc in next lp, 2 dc in next lp] twice, turn. *(15 dc)*

Continue with For All Sizes.

For Size Large Only

Row 1: Hold Back with RS facing you and beg ch at top, skip next 21 unused lps of beg ch from Right Front Shoulder, join in next lp, ch 3, dc in same lp, dc in next lp, ch 1, sk next lp, 2 dc in next lp, dc in next lp, [ch 1, sk next lp, dc in next 3 lps] twice, [ch 1, sk next lp, dc in next lp, 2 dc in next lp] twice, turn. *(18 dc)*

Continue with For All Sizes.

For Size X-large Only

Row 1: Hold Back with RS facing you and beg ch at top, skip next 21 unused lps of beg ch from Right Front Shoulder, join in next lp, ch 3, 2 dc in next lp, [ch 1, sk next lp, dc in next lp, 2 dc in next lp] 5 times, ch 1, sk next lp, dc in next 3 lps, turn. *(21 dc)*

Continue with For All Sizes.

For Size 2X Only

Row 1: Hold Back with RS facing you and beg ch at top, skip next 21 unused lps of beg ch from Right Front Shoulder, join in next lp, ch 3, 2 dc in next lp, [ch 1, sk next lp, dc in next lp, 2 dc in next lp] 7 times, turn. *(24 dc)*

Continue with For All Sizes.

For All Sizes

Row 2: Ch 1, sc in first dc, *ch 4, sc in next ch-1 sp, rep from * to last 2 dc and beg ch-3; ch 4, sk last 2 dc, sc in 3rd ch of beg ch-3, turn. *(5 [6, 7, 8, 9] sc)*

Row 3: Sl st in next ch-4 sp, ch 3, 2 dc in same sp, *ch 1, 3 dc in next ch-4 sp, rep from * across; turn. *(12 (15, 18, 21, 24] dc)*

Rows 4–9 [4–9, 4–9, 4–11, 4–11]: [Work rows 2 and 3] 3 [3, 3, 4, 4] times.

Row 10 [10, 10, 12, 12]: Ch 1, sc in first dc, *ch 4, sc in next ch-1 sp, rep from * to last ch-1 sp; turn, leaving rem sts unworked. *(4 [5, 6, 7, 8] sc)*

Row 11 [11, 11, 13, 13]: Rep row 3. *(9 [12, 15, 18, 21] dc)*

Row 12 [12, 12, 14, 14]: Rep row 10 [10, 10, 12, 12]. *(3 [4, 5, 6, 7] sc)*

Row 13 [13, 13, 15, 15]: Rep row 3. *(6 [9, 12, 15, 18] dc)*

Fasten off and weave in ends.

Underarm Seam

Matching up edges of rows, sew last 2 rows of front panels to corresponding rows on Back.

Sleeve

Make 2.

Rnd 1: Hold piece with RS facing you, make slip knot on hook and join with sc in outer edge of foundation ch on back (shoulder seam), working in edges of first 11 [11, 11, 13, 13] rows on Front Shoulders and first 11 [11, 11, 13, 13] rows of Back (armhole opening), sk next row, ch 4, [sc in next row, sk next row, ch 4] 5 [5, 5, 6, 6] times, sc in underarm seam, sk next row, ch 4, [sc in next row, sk next row, ch 4] 5 [5, 5, 6, 6] times, join in first sc. *(12 [12, 12, 14, 14] ch-4 sps)*

Rnd 2: Sl st in next ch-4 sp, ch 4 *(counts as a tr)*, 2 tr in same sp, ch 1, *3 tr in next ch-4 sp, ch 1, rep from * around; join in 4th ch of beg ch-4. *(36 [36, 36, 42, 42] tr)*

Rnd 3: Ch 1, sc in same ch as joining, ch 4, *sc in next ch-1 sp, ch 4, rep from * around; join in first sc. *(12 (12, 12, 14, 14] ch-4 sps)*

Rnds 4–17: [Work rnds 2 and 3] 7 times.

For Sizes Small, Medium, & Large only

Fasten off and weave in ends.

Continue with Collar.

For Sizes X-large & 2X only

Rnd 18: Rep rnd 2.

Fasten off and weave in ends.

Continue with Collar.

Collar

Note: *With tapestry needle, string paillettes on yarn.*

Rnd 1: Hold piece with RS facing you and unworked section of beg ch at top, make slip knot on hook and join with sc in sp formed by first sk ch of beg ch from Right Front Shoulder, [ch 4, sc in sp formed by next sk ch] 5 times, working in ends of rows on Left Front Shoulder, [ch 4, sk next dc row, sc in next sc row] 4 [4, 4, 5, 5] times, ch 4, sc in top of next dc row, [ch 4, sk next sc row, sc in top of next dc row] twice, ch 4, working across last row of Left Front Shoulder, [sc in next ch-1 sp, ch 4] 1 [2, 3, 4, 5] times, sk next 2 dc, sc in next dc, working in ends of rows of Back, [sc in next sc row, ch 4, sk next dc row] twice,[sc in next sc row, ch 4, sc in top of next dc row, ch 4] 4 times, working across last row of Back, [sc in next ch-1 sp, ch 4] 6 [7, 8, 9, 10] times, sk next 2 dc, sc in next dc, working across next side in ends of rows, [ch 4, sc in next sc row, ch 4, sc in top of next dc row] 4 times, ch 4, sc in next sc row and in next dc on Right Front Shoulder, [ch 4, sc in next ch-1 sp] 1 [2, 3, 4, 5] times, ch 4, sk next 2 dc, sc in next dc, working in ends of rows of Right Front Shoulder, [ch 4, sc in next sc row, ch 4, sc in top of next dc row] twice, ch 4, sc in next sc row, [ch 4, sk next dc row, sc in next sc row] 3 [3, 3, 4, 4] times, ch 4, sk next dc row, join in first sc. (*50 [53, 56, 61, 64] ch-4 sps*)

Rnd 2: Sl st in next ch-4 sp, ch 4 (*counts as a tr*), 2 tr in same sp, ch 1, *****3 tr in next ch-4 sp, ch 1, rep from ***** around; join in 4th ch of beg ch-4. (*150 [159, 168, 183, 192] tr*)

Rnd 3: Ch 1, sc in same ch as joining, ch 4, *****sc in next ch-1 sp, ch 4, rep from ***** around; join in first sc. (*50 [53, 56, 61, 64] ch-4 sps*)

Rnds 4 & 5: Rep rnds 2 and 3.

Rnd 6: Sl st in next ch-4 sp, ch 3, slide paillette up, ch 1 (*counts as beg* ***paillette tr***), 2 paillette tr (*see Special Stitch*) in same sp, ch 1, [3 paillette tr in next ch-4 sp, ch 1] 14 times, [3 tr in next ch-4 sp, ch 1] 25 [28, 31, 36, 39] times, [3 paillette tr in next ch-4 sp, ch 1] 10 times, join in ch after first paillette.

Rnd 7: Rep rnd 3.

Rnd 8: Rep rnd 6.

Rnd 9: Rep rnd 3.

Rnd 10: Rep rnd 6.

Fasten off and weave in ends.

Standard Yarn Weight System

Categories of yarn, gauge ranges, and recommended needle and hook sizes

Yarn Weight Symbol & Category Names	1 SUPER FINE	2 FINE	3 LIGHT	4 MEDIUM	5 BULKY	6 SUPER BULKY
Type of Yarns in Category	Sock, Fingering, Baby	Sport, Baby	DK, Light Worsted	Worsted, Afghan, Aran	Chunky, Craft, Rug	Bulky, Roving
Crochet Gauge* Ranges in Single Crochet to 4 inch	21–32 sts	16–20 sts	12–17 sts	11–14 sts	8–11 sts	5–9 sts
Recommended Hook in Metric Size Range	2.25–3.5 mm	3.5–4.5 mm	4.5–5.5 mm	5.5–6.5 mm	6.5–9 mm	9 mm and larger
Recommended Hook U.S. Size Range	B1–E4	E4–7	7–I-9	I-9–K-10½	K-10½–M-13	M-13 and larger

* GUIDELINES ONLY: The above reflect the most commonly used gauges and hook sizes for specific yarn categories.

Abbreviations & Symbols

beg .... begin/beginning
bpdc .... back post double crochet
bpsc .... back post single crochet
bptr .... back post treble crochet
CC .... contrasting color
ch .... chain stitch
ch- .... refers to chain or space previously made (i.e. ch-1 space)
ch sp .... chain space
cl .... cluster
cm .... centimeter(s)
dc .... double crochet
dc dec .... double crochet 2 or more stitches together, as indicated
dec .... decrease/decreases/decreasing
dtr .... double treble crochet
fpdc .... front post double crochet
fpsc .... front post single crochet
fptr .... front post treble crochet
g .... grams
hdc .... half double crochet
hdc dec ... half double crochet 2 or more stitches together, as indicated
lp(s) .... loops(s)
MC .... main color
mm .... millimeter(s)
oz .... ounce(s)
pc .... popcorn
rem .... remain/remaining
rep .... repeat(s)
rnd(s) .... round(s)
RS .... right side
sc .... single crochet
sc dec .... single crochet 2 or more stitches together, as indicated
sk .... skip
sl st .... slip stitch
sp(s) .... space(s)
st(s) .... stitch(es)
tog .... together
tr .... treble crochet
trtr .... triple treble
WS .... wrong side
yd(s) .... yard(s)
yo .... yarn over

* An asterisk (or double asterisk **) is used to mark the beginning of a portion of instructions to be worked more than once; thus, "rep from * twice more" means after working the instructions once, repeat the instructions following the asterisk twice more (3 times in all).

[] Brackets are used to enclose instructions that should be worked the exact number of times specified immediately following the brackets, such as "[2 sc in next dc, sc in next dc] twice." They are also used to set off and clarify a group of stitches that are to be worked all into the same space or stitch, such as "in next corner sp work [2 dc, ch 1, 2 dc]."

[] Brackets and () parentheses are used to provide additional information to clarify instructions.

Join—join with a sl st unless otherwise specified.

The patterns in this book are written using United States terminology. Terms that have different British equivalents are noted below.

U.S. Terms	U.K. Terms
single crochet (sc)	double crochet (dc)
double crochet (dc)	treble (tr)
treble crochet (tr)	double treble (dtr)
skip (sk)	miss
slip stitch (sl st)	slip stitch (ss) or single crochet
gauge	tension
yarn over (yo)	yarn over hook (YOH)

How to Check Gauge

A correct stitch gauge is very important. Please take the time to work a stitch gauge swatch about 4 x 4 inches. Measure the swatch. If the number of stitches and rows are fewer than indicated under "Gauge" in the pattern, your hook is too large. Try another swatch with a smaller size hook. If the number of stitches and rows are more than indicated under "Gauge" in the pattern, your hook is too small. Try another swatch with a larger size hook.

Stitch Guide

Chain—ch:
YO, draw through lp on hook.

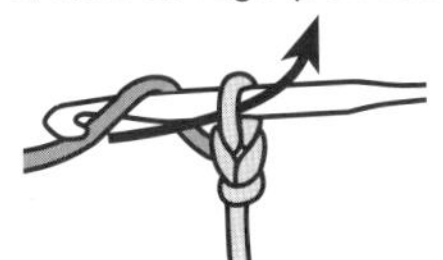

Single Crochet—sc:
Insert hook in st, yo and draw through, yo and draw through both lps on hook.

Reverse Single Crochet—Reverse sc:
Work from left to right, insert hook in sp or st indicated (**a**), draw lp through sp or st - 2 lps on hook (**b**); yo and draw through lps on hook.

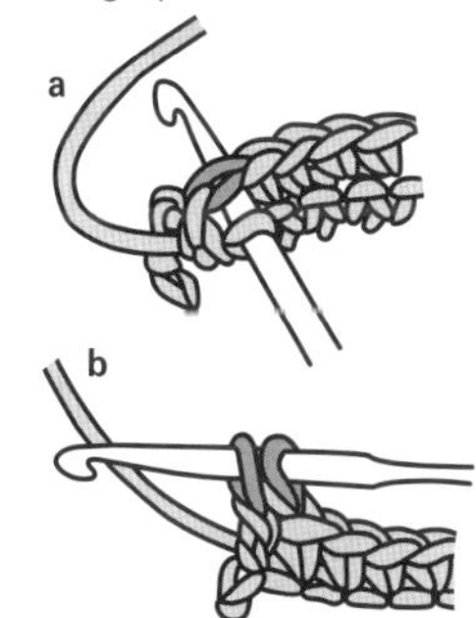

Half Double Crochet—hdc:
yo, insert hook in st, yo, draw through, yo and draw through all 3 lps on hook.

Double Crochet—dc:
yo, insert hook in st, yo, draw through, (yo and draw through 2 lps on hook) twice.

Triple Crochet—trc:
yo twice, insert hook in st, yo, draw through, (yo and draw through 2 lps on hook) 3 times.

Slip Stitch—sl st:
(**a**) **Used for Joinings**
Insert hook in indicated st, yo and draw through st and lp on hook.

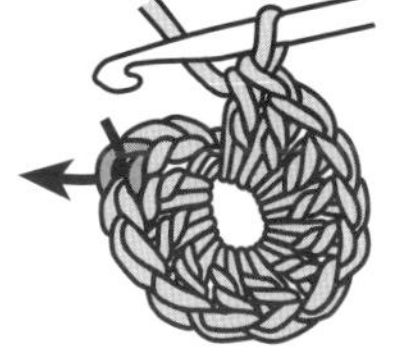

(**b**) **Used for Moving Yarn Over**
Insert hook in st, yo draw through st and lp on hook.

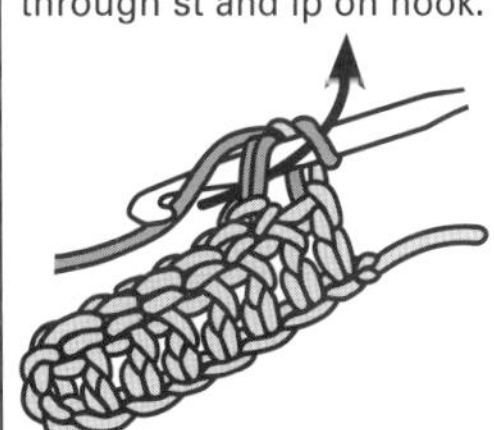

Front Loop—FL:
The front loop is the loop toward you at the top of the stitch.

Back Loop—BL:
The back loop is the loop away from you at the top of the stitch.

Post:
The post is the vertical part of the stitch.

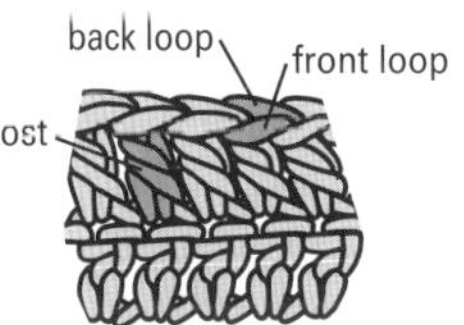

Overcast Stitch is worked loosely to join crochet pieces.

Skill Levels

BEGINNER
Beginner projects for first-time crocheters using basic stitches. Minimal shaping.

EASY
Easy projects using basic stitches, repetitive stitch patterns, simple color changes and simple shaping and finishing.

INTERMEDIATE
Intermediate projects with a variety of stitches, mid-level shaping and finishing.

EXPERIENCED
Experienced projects using advanced techniques and stitches, detailed shaping and refined finishing.

Metric Charts

INCHES INTO MILLIMETERS & CENTIMETERS (Rounded off slightly)

inches	mm	cm	inches	cm	inches	cm	inches	cm
1/8	3	0.3	5	12.5	21	53.5	38	96.5
1/4	6	0.6	5 1/2	14	22	56	39	99
3/8	10	1	6	15	23	58.5	40	101.5
1/2	13	1.3	7	18	24	61	41	104
5/8	15	1.5	8	20.5	25	63.5	42	106.5
3/4	20	2	9	23	26	66	43	109
7/8	22	2.2	10	25.5	27	68.5	44	112
1	25	2.5	11	28	28	71	45	114.5
1 1/4	32	3.2	12	30.5	29	73.5	46	117
1 1/2	38	3.8	13	33	30	76	47	119.5
1 3/4	45	4.5	14	35.5	31	79	48	122
2	50	5	15	38	32	81.5	49	124.5
2 1/2	65	6.5	16	40.5	33	84	50	127
3	75	7.5	17	43	34	86.5		
3 1/2	90	9	18	46	35	89		
4	100	10	19	48.5	36	91.5		
4 1/2	115	11.5	20	51	37	94		

CROCHET HOOKS CONVERSION CHART

U.S.	1/B	2/C	3/D	4/E	5/F	6/G	8/H	9/I	10/J	10½/K	N
Continental-mm	2.25	2.75	3.25	3.5	3.75	4.25	5	5.5	6	6.5	9.0

STEELTHREAD HOOKS METRIC CONVERSION CHART

U.S.	16	14	13	12	11	10	9	8	7	6	5	4	3	2	1	0	00
U.K.	-	7	6½	6	5½	5	4	3	2½	2	1½	1	1/0	2/0	3/0	00	-
Metric-mm	0.6	0.75	0.85	1.00	1.10	1.15	1.25	1.50	1.65	1.80	1.90	2.00	2.10	2.20	2.25	2.50	2.70

DRG Publishing
306 East Parr Road
Berne, IN 46711

TOLL-FREE ORDER LINE or to request a free catalog (800) 582-6643
Customer Service (800) 282-6643, **Fax** (800) 882-6643

Visit AnniesAttic.com.

ISBN-10: 1-59012-165-1
ISBN-13: 978-1-59012-165-8

Printed in USA

1 2 3 4 5 6 7 8 9